Introduction

This book has been created from the drawings of Nathan Russel. Nathan is 19 years old and autistic. He attends Debbi's Doodles where he works with Neil Cole from The Museum of Classic Sci-fi in Northumberland to create his works of art.

We hope you enjoy this colouring book.

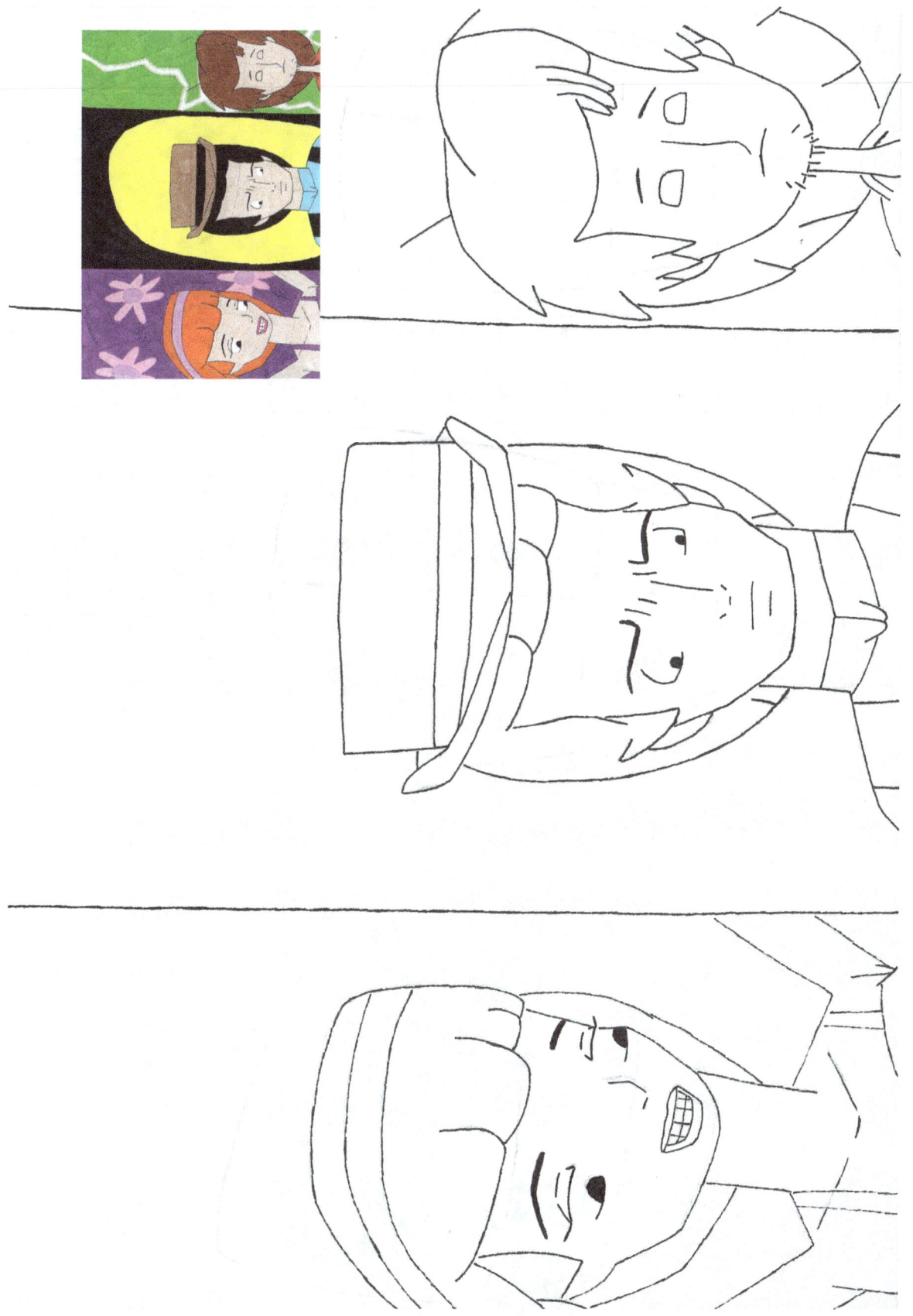

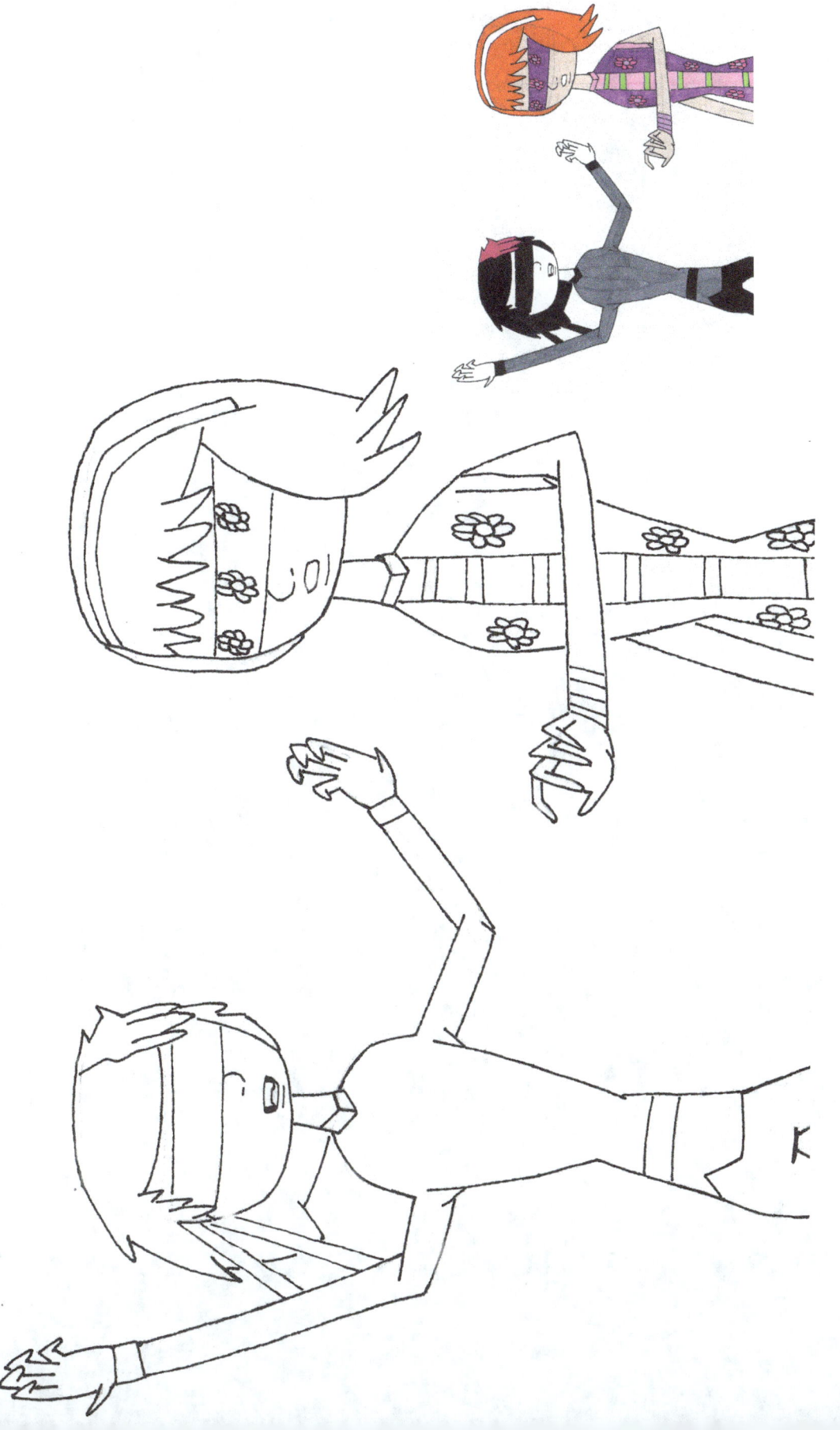

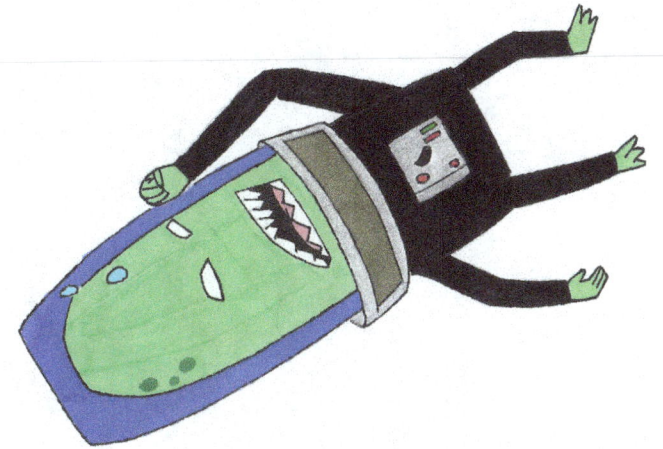
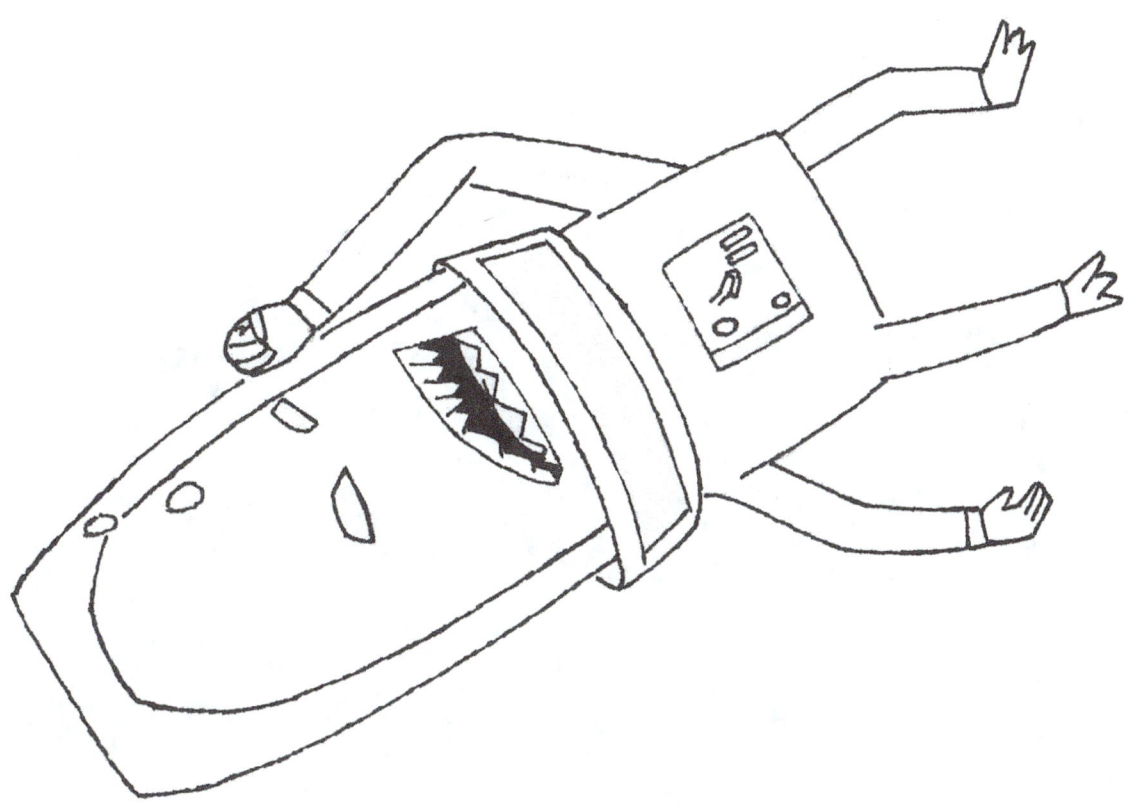

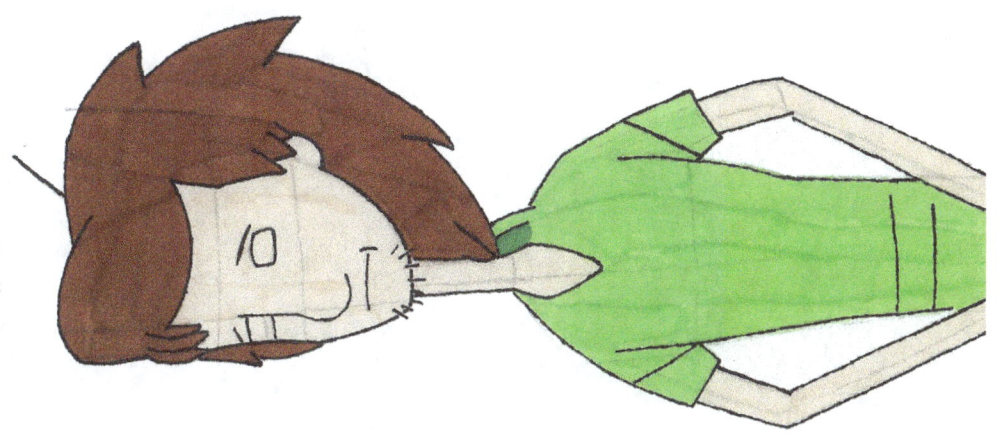

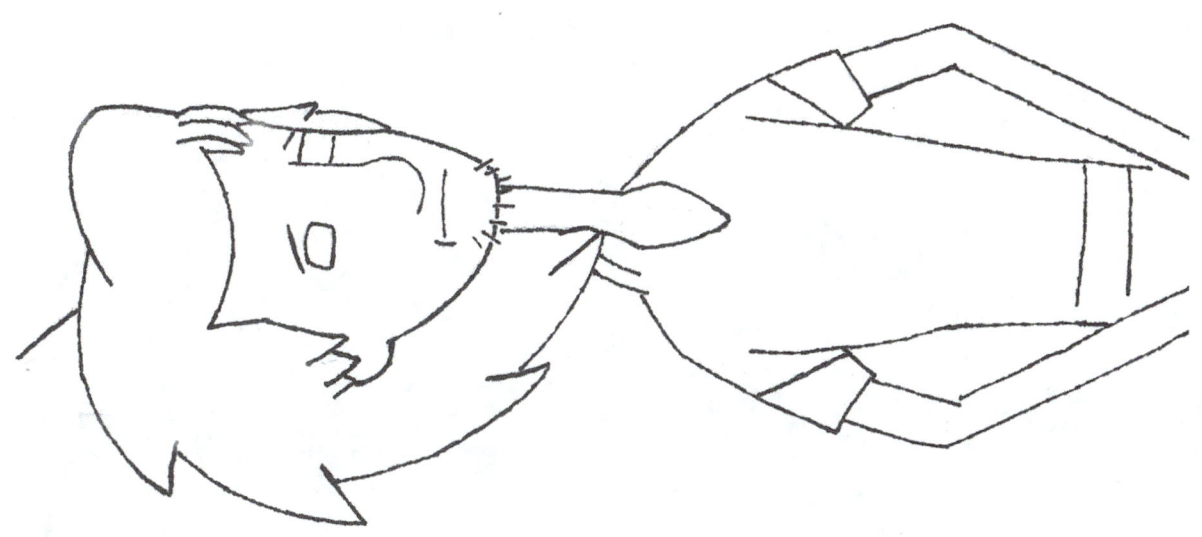

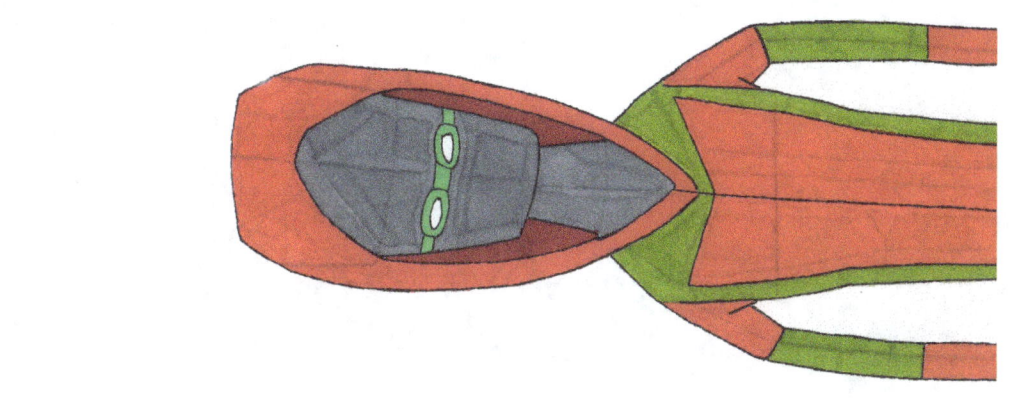

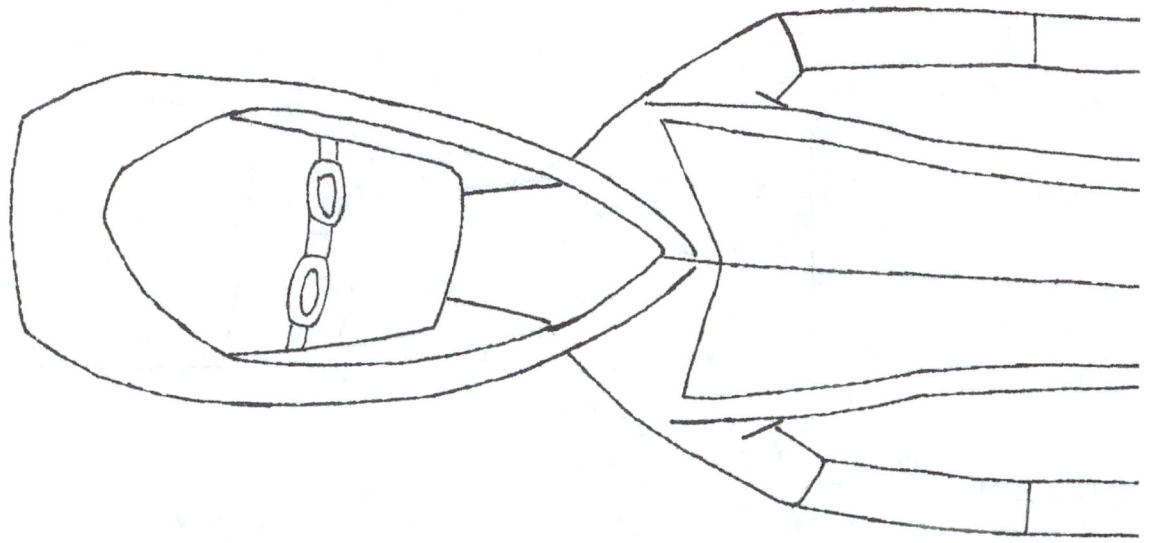

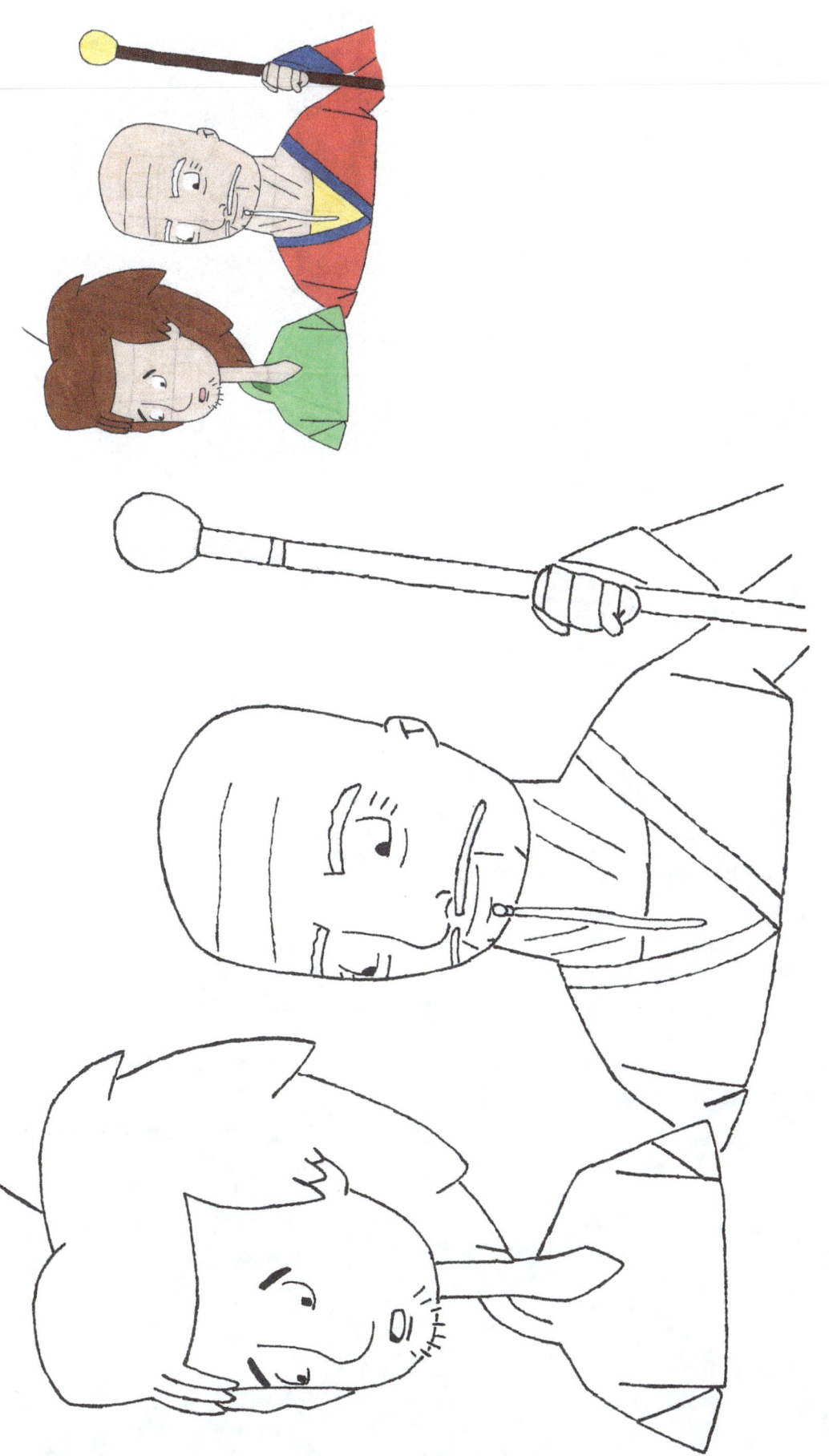

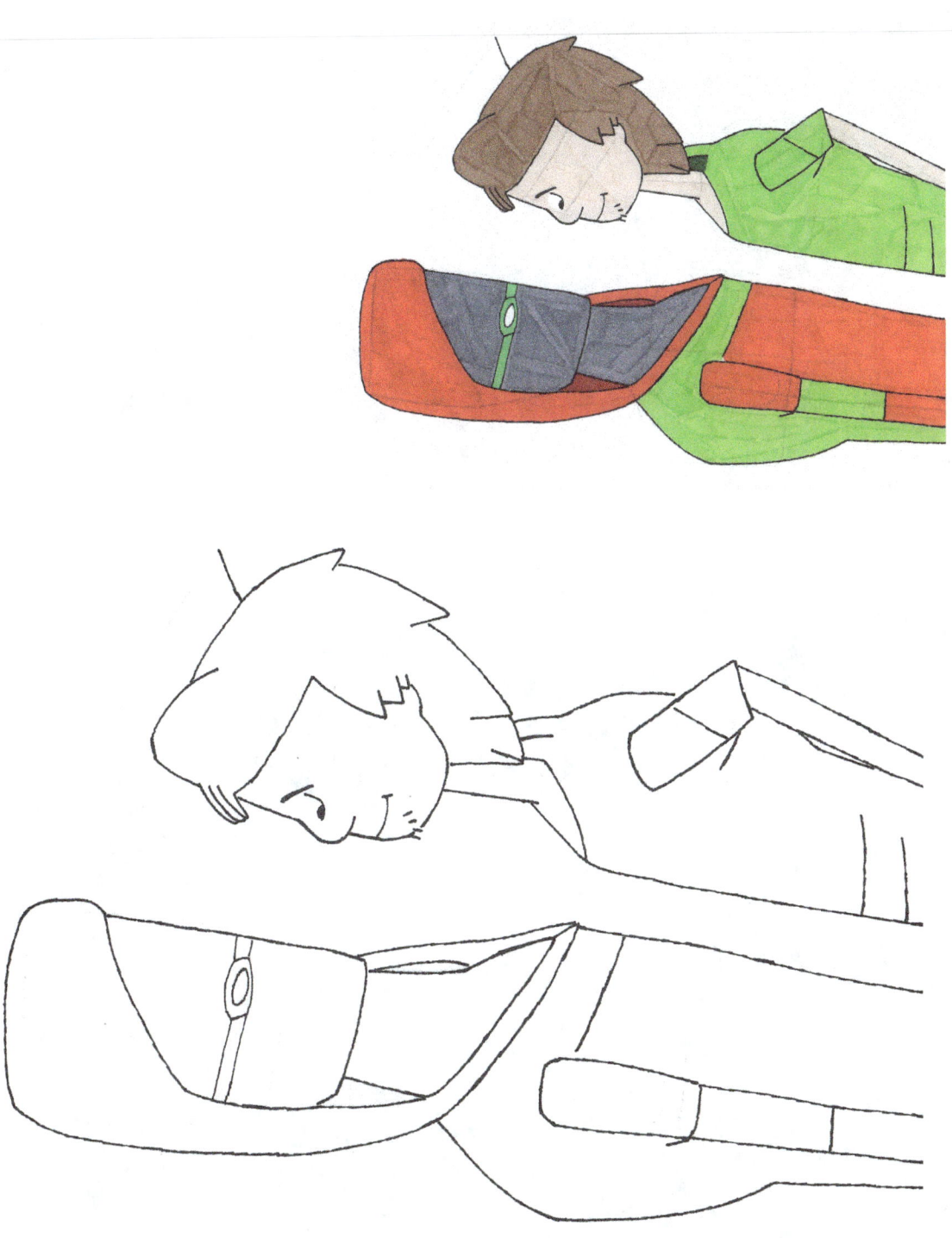

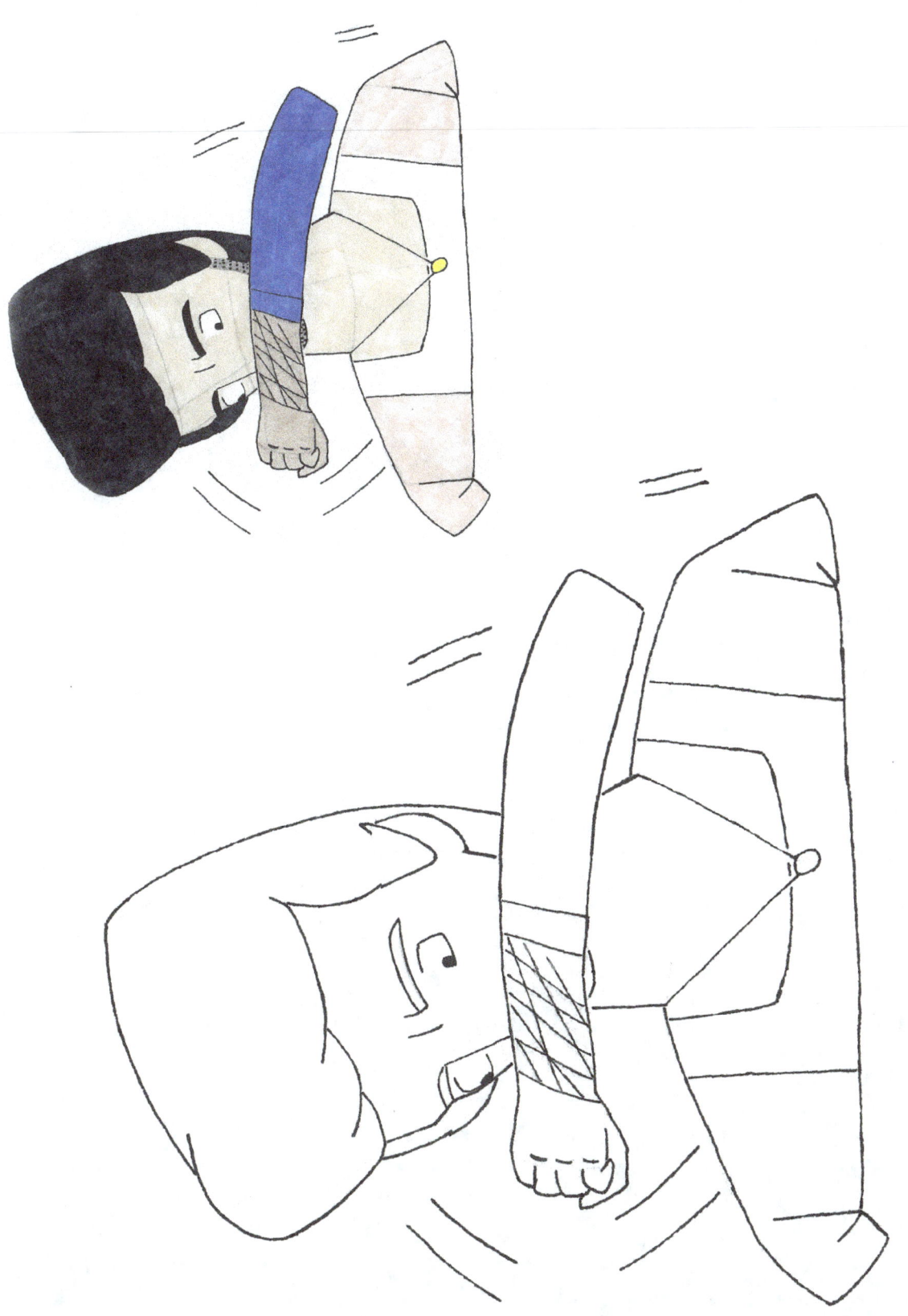

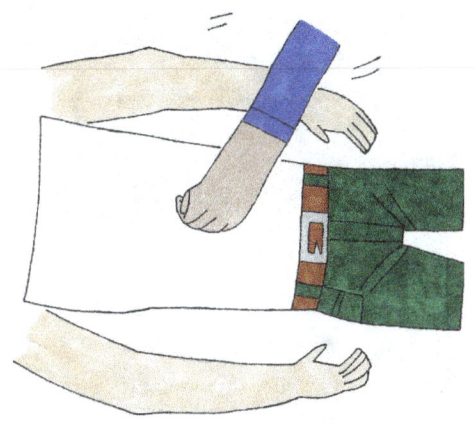

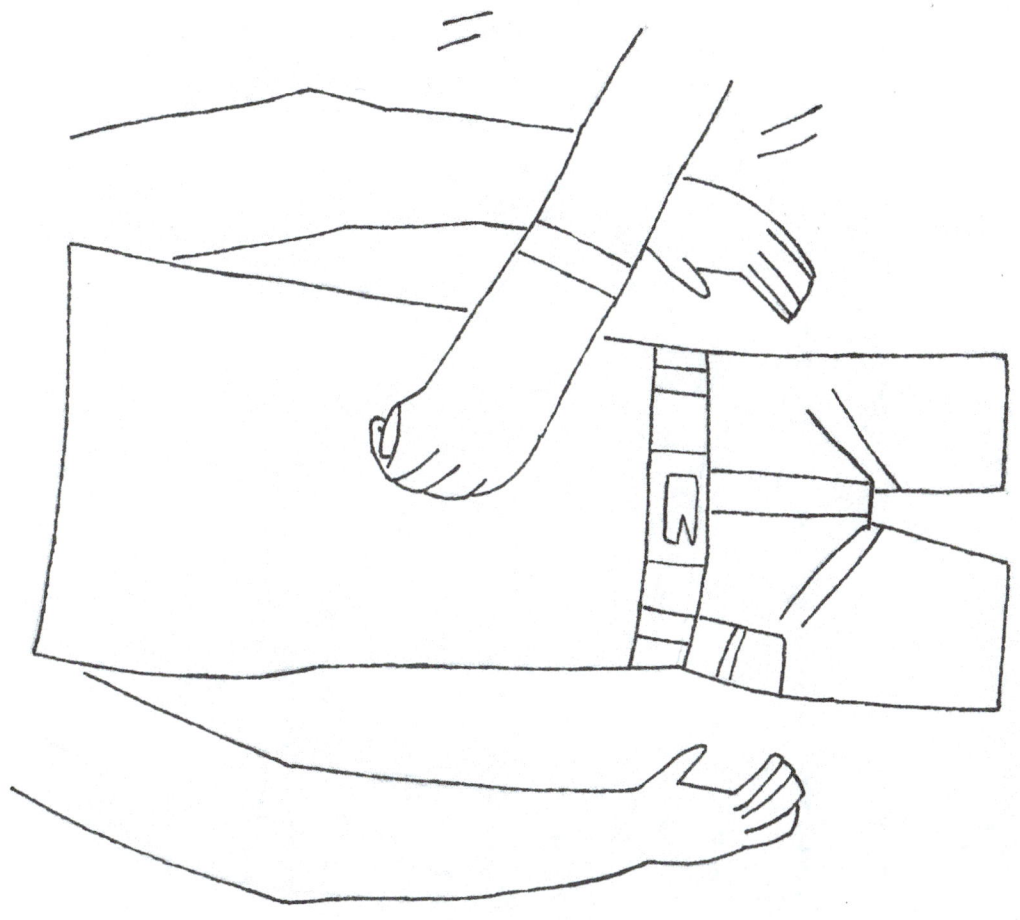

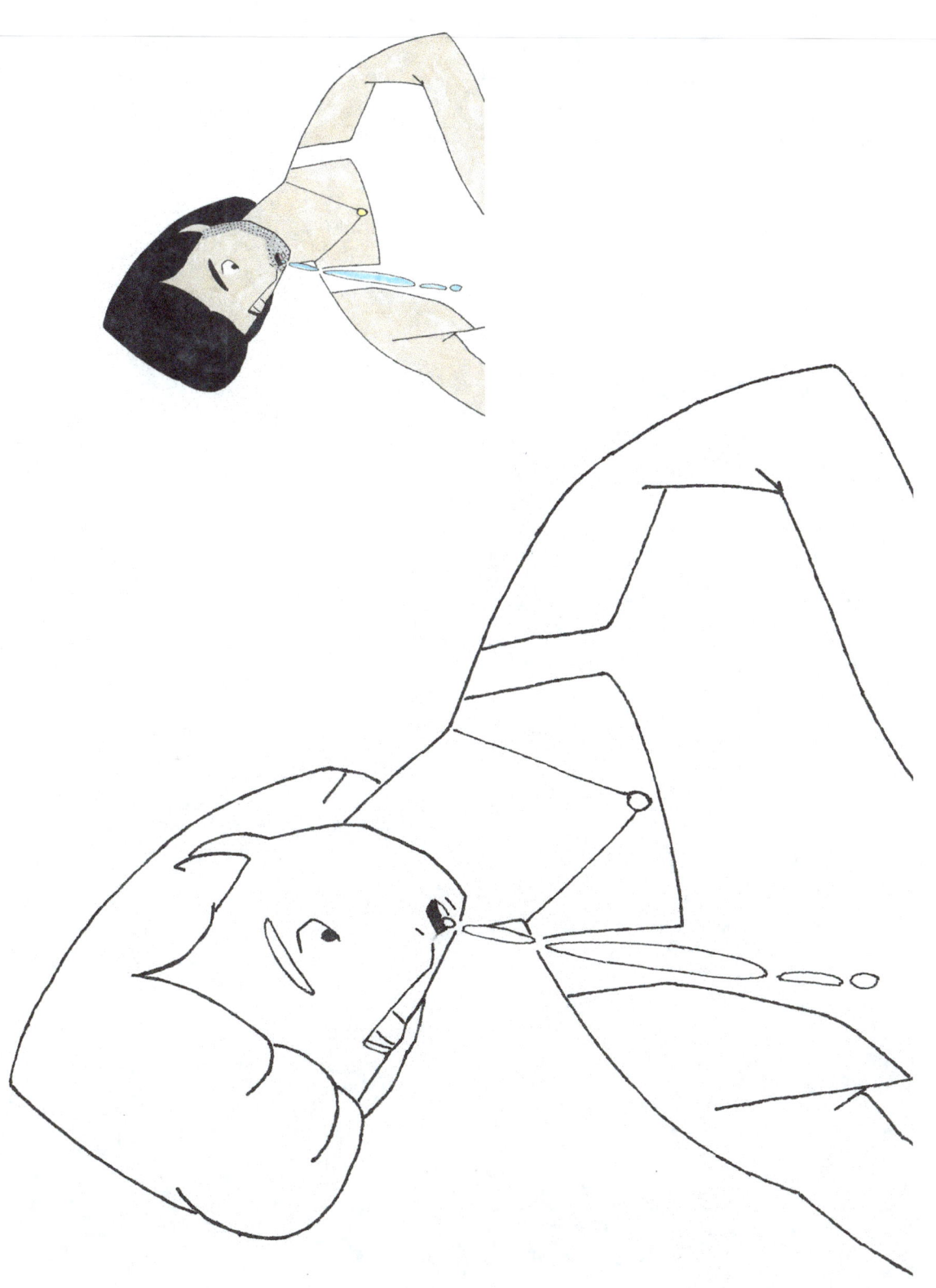

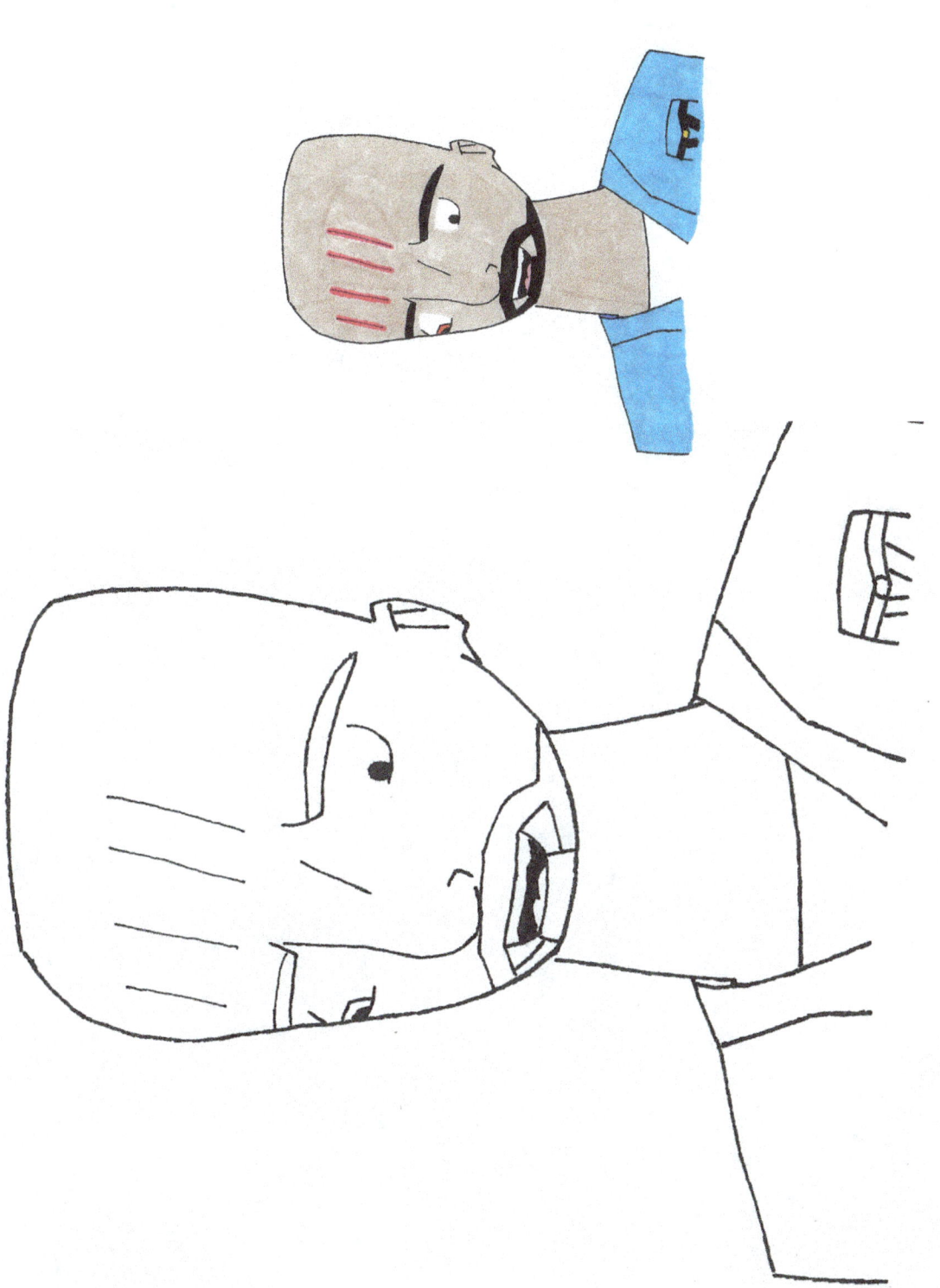

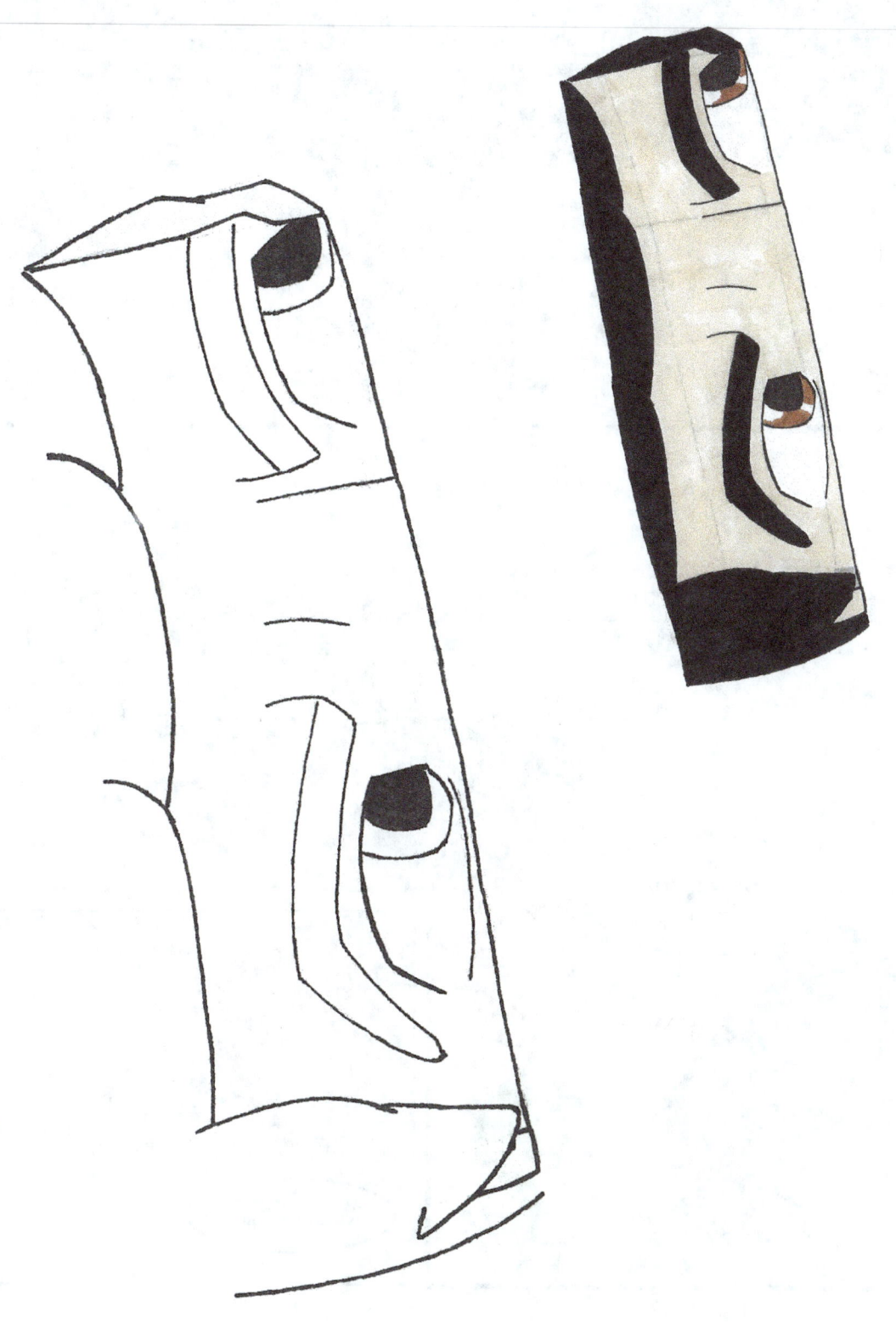